The Jesus Tree

48 Family Devotions For Lent

~ Stories from Jesus' Life ~

~ Prayers & Questions ~

Anna Sklar

The Jesus Tree—48 Family Devotions for Lent

Copyright © 2017 by Anna Sklar

All rights reserved. Without limiting the rights under copyright reserved above, no part of this publication may be reproduced, stored in or introduced into a retrieval system, or transmitted, in any form, or by any means (electronic, mechanical, photocopying, recording, or otherwise) without the prior written permission of the copyright owner of this book.

ISBN-13: 978-1540460370

ISBN-10: 1540460371

Books may be purchased online:

Createspace.com

Amazon sites worldwide

Digital Downloads available on Etsy:

https://www.etsy.com/ca/shop/SklarInk

Contact the author at:

Simply Live Blog—*annasklar.ca*

Etsy Shop—*SklarInk—etsy.com/ca/shop/SklarInk*

To Jesus

For wandering in the wilderness of our lives
Helping us resist temptation
Giving us wisdom and strength
Showing us truth
Loving us beyond all reason
Lifting our burdens
Carrying our crosses
Taking our sin
Opening our hearts
To all that You are

Thank You

What is Lent?
Lent is a special time of year. It leads us right up to Easter and helps us focus on Jesus' life, death, and resurrection. Many people choose to give up something for Lent, to help them remember Jesus giving up his life for us on the cross. Others practice Lent by doing something kind for people every day. There are many ideas for making Lent a wonderful time with your family.

What is The Jesus Tree?
The Jesus Tree is one of those wonderful ideas I just mentioned! I've put together a set of 48 daily devotions for your family to use during this season of Lent. Included each day is a story from Jesus' life, a scripture reading, a discussion question, and a prayer. These devotions can be made into ornaments to hang on a tree, or an Easter garland, or wherever you like! Your family will learn all about Jesus' life - from birth to resurrection. Watch your family's faith grow as *The Jesus Tree* grows!

How To Use The Jesus Tree Family Devotions
On the first day of Lent (Ash Wednesday), read the first story in *The Jesus Tree* book. Children can turn to the scripture passage in their Bible if they are old enough. Discuss the question(s) in the *Talk About* section and read the prayer with the children. Do this every day during the season of Lent, in numerical order, finishing up on Easter Monday.

You can also encourage the children to lead the Jesus Tree devotions with your family.

CONTENTS

1.	Ash Wednesday	8
2.	Jesus' Parents	9
3.	The Birth of Jesus	10
4.	Jesus' First Visit to the Temple	11
5.	Escape to Egypt	12
6.	Another Visit to the Temple	13
7.	Jesus the Carpenter	14
8.	Jesus the Son	15
9.	Jesus the Brother & Friend	16
10.	Jesus the Cousin & John's Story	17
11.	Baptism of Jesus	18
12.	Jesus in the Wilderness	19
13.	First Miracle of Jesus	20
14.	Nicodemus	21
15.	Jesus Heals a Nobleman's Son	22
16.	Four Fishermen Follow Jesus	23
17.	Matthew Follows Jesus	24
18.	Jesus Chooses 12 Disciples	25
19.	Sermon on the Mount	26
20.	Parables of Jesus	27

21.	Jesus Calms the Storm	28
22.	Nazareth Turns Against Jesus	29
23.	Jesus Sends Out the 12	30
24.	Jesus Feeds Thousands!	31
25.	Jesus Walks on Water	32
26.	Jesus Says He Will Die Soon	33
27.	Jesus Transforms on the Mountain	34
28.	Jesus Sends Out the 72	35
29.	Jesus Attends A Feast	36
30.	Jesus Raises Lazarus from the Dead	37
31.	Jesus Spends Time Alone with God	38
32.	The Great Commandments	39
33.	We Need to Really Love Them…	40
34.	The Parable of the Good Samaritan	41
35.	Jesus Washes the Disciples' Feet	42
36.	Jesus Blesses the Children	43
37.	Zacchaeus Climbs a Tree	44
38.	Jesus Arrives at Bethany	45
39.	The Sabbath	46
40.	Holy Week Begins—Palm Sunday	47
41.	Monday—Jesus Clears the Temple	48

42.	Tuesday—Two Coins	49
43.	Wednesday—Perfume Poured on Jesus	50
44.	Thursday—Communion & the Garden	51
45.	Good Friday—Crucifixion	52
46.	Saturday—Jesus in the Tomb	53
47.	Easter Sunday—Resurrection	54
48.	Easter Monday	55
	About the Author	56
	Other Resources by Anna	57

1. Ash Wednesday

Lent is a special time of the year. It starts 48 days before Easter and it's a time to really think about Jesus. Do you know the story of Easter? Do you know about the life of Jesus? We'll be learning about it together during Lent - starting today! Today is the first day of Lent and it's called Ash Wednesday. On this day people around the world think about the cross. At the end of Jesus' life on earth He died on a cross, but that's not the end of His story! Do you know the end of His story? If not, you'll be amazed when we learn about it together! But for now, let's get back to Ash Wednesday. Some people have a cross of ashes drawn on their forehead or make a painting out of ashes. The ashes remind us of death - the death of Jesus and the death of our sins. Tomorrow we'll start looking at the LIFE of Jesus - he did many amazing things!

Talk About: What do you know about Lent so far? What about Jesus?

Prayer: Lord, let us learn many new things about you this Lent season.

2. Jesus' Parents

Read: Luke 1:26-38, Matthew 1:18-25

Do you know about King David in the Bible? Well, his great, great, great, great (say great 20 more times) grandson was Joseph. Joseph was engaged to be married to a young lady named Mary. Before the wedding, God asked Mary to grow a baby boy inside her. This baby would be the most special baby of all time. He would be Jesus - the Messiah - the one who saves people from sin. Mary said yes to God and a tiny, tiny baby started to grow in Mary. God can do amazing things like that! Joseph wasn't sure if he was still supposed to be Mary's husband, so God sent an angel to tell Joseph that he was supposed to be Mary's husband and Jesus' father. Joseph was a good man. Both Mary and Joseph loved God very much and did their best to follow Him all their lives.

Talk About: Do you know the names of your great-grandparents?

Prayer: Thank you for all the people that love me in my life.

3. The Birth of Jesus

Read: Luke 2:1-21

When the time came for Jesus to be born, His parents were travelling to Bethlehem, the town of King David, in Judea. All the hotels and motels were full, but they were told they could stay in a stable with the animals. That's where Jesus was born - in a stable! Shepherds in a nearby field saw angels appear in the sky, telling them about the birth of Jesus. They knew this must be a very important child if angels were singing and talking to them! So the shepherds rushed off to see the baby and they praised God for Him.

Talk About: How do you think you would feel if you saw angels singing in the sky? What about if the angels started TALKING to you?

Prayer: God, thank you for sending Jesus to earth. It must have been strange to be born in a stable instead of a hospital, so thank you that Jesus was safe and warm there. Thank you for special things like angels. I'm glad the angels told the shepherds about baby Jesus, and now I get to read about it in the Bible!

4. Jesus' First Visit to the Temple

Read: Luke 2:22-40

When Jesus was only a few days old, his parents took him to the temple (church) in Jerusalem. There they met Simeon - a man who had been waiting his whole life to meet the Messiah. He was so happy to finally meet Jesus. Simeon held baby Jesus in his arms and blessed Mary and Joseph.

There was also a woman named Anna at the temple who prayed and worshipped God ALL THE TIME. She was 84 years old and she had only been married 7 years before her husband died. So she spent most of her life at the temple. She thanked God for Jesus and told everyone about him.

There were many people who had been waiting for the Messiah to be born!

Talk About: Can you imagine waiting your whole life to meet someone? Or spending your days praying at church? What would that feel like?

Prayer: Help us to meet special people at church who can be good friends in our lives & help us get to know you more. We would love to meet people we can laugh with when things are happy or cry with when things are sad.

5. Escape to Egypt

Read: Matthew 2:13-21

Wise Men came to visit Jesus after he was born. They gave Jesus gifts of gold, frankincense, and myrrh. The Wise Men told the king of Judea about Jesus, and the king didn't like the idea of a "Messiah". He didn't want someone else helping his people or saving them or being called a leader to them. So he ordered that all boys two years old and younger would be killed! God is so amazing and powerful that He knew about all of this and sent an angel to warn Joseph. Joseph took Mary and Jesus and escaped to Egypt until a few years later when mean King Herod died. Then God sent another angel to Joseph to tell him it was safe to come back to the land of Israel. They went to live in a town called Nazareth.

Talk About: Has anyone ever tried to hurt you?

Prayer: Thank you for watching over us and for sending your angels to protect us sometimes. Even though we can't see them, we know they are there to look out for us.

6. Another Visit to the Temple

Read: Luke 2:41-52

Every year Jesus' parents went to Jerusalem for the Passover Feast. When Jesus was 12 years old, they went to the feast as usual. After the feast, Jesus' parents left to go back home. The boy Jesus stayed behind in Jerusalem, but his parents didn't know he had stayed! They thought he was travelling in their group of family and friends! They travelled for a whole day before they realized Jesus was not with them! Mary and Joseph began to look for Jesus in their group, but they couldn't find him. So they went back to Jerusalem to look for him. After THREE DAYS they found him in the temple courtyard. He was sitting with the teachers, listening to them, and asking them questions. Everyone who heard him was amazed at how much he understood about God. Jesus' parents were upset with him, but "He went back to Nazareth with them, and He obeyed them."

Talk About: Have you ever been lost?

Prayer: We always want to follow where you want us to go God!

7. Jesus the Carpenter

Read: Mark 6:3

Remember that Jesus' father was named Joseph? Joseph's job was to be a carpenter. This means that he worked with wood - building and fixing things for the people in his neighbourhood. Sons used to learn all about how to do their father's jobs, so Jesus was taught by Joseph to be a carpenter. Girls usually learned many things from their mothers about taking care of a house and raising children.

Jesus and Joseph spent many hours together in the workshop. Jesus learned everything his father knew about working with wood. I bet Jesus loved being in the workshop, creating chairs or tables or beds. And I bet he was very handy to have around if you needed something to be built or fixed!

Talk About: What jobs does your family do? Would you like to do those jobs?

Prayer: Show us the jobs you have for us to do every day. Show us the work you want us to do and the people you want us to help.

8. Jesus the Son

Read: Luke 2:32-40

Jesus was God's son - God did a very special thing when He placed a tiny, tiny baby Jesus inside of Mary so He could grow and be born like any other baby. But He wasn't like any other baby at all. He was specially made by God to do the really special job of saving people from sin. Sin is all the wrong things we do and the mistakes we make in our lives.

Mary and Joseph raised Jesus as their son and taught Him to be a kind, gentle, hard-working man who knew all about His Father in heaven. They took Jesus to the temple and celebrated all their Jewish holidays with Him. The Bible says "And the child grew and became strong; he was filled with wisdom, and the grace of God was on him." Luke 2:40 "And Jesus grew in wisdom and stature, and in favour with God and man." Luke 2:52

Talk About: What does it mean to be wise and in favour with God?

Prayer: As we grow up and get older, help us grow more and more into people that make you happy.

9. Jesus the Brother & Friend

Read: Matthew 13:54-58

The Bible tells us that Jesus was the first child of a large family. He had at least four brothers - James, Joseph, Simon, and Judas. Jesus also had a few sisters, but we're not sure of how many or what their names were.

Can you imagine having Jesus as your older brother? He always did HIs best to follow everything God asked Him to do, so He would have been a very fun, kind, and loving brother. He must have had so much fun as He was growing up, playing with all his brothers and sisters, helping with the new babies, eating and laughing at the dinner table, and sleeping peacefully in a room shared by many of the people in his family.

Talk About: How many people are in your family? What is the most fun part of being in your family?

Prayer: Help me be kind, loving, fun and helpful with my friends and the people in my family. I hope the things I do will show them about your love for everyone.

10. Jesus the Cousin & John's Story

Read: Luke 1:5-25, 57-66

Jesus had a cousin who was born a few months before Him. His name was John (many people call him John the Baptist because he was the first one to baptize people). John's father was a priest named Zechariah. Part of the job of a priest was to go to the temple and pray for the people. An angel appeared to Zechariah in the temple one day and told him he would have a son. The angel said to name the son John. Zechariah didn't believe the angel because he and his wife were very old. The angel told Zechariah he wouldn't be able to speak until the baby was born because he didn't believe the news about baby John! Sure enough, Zechariah and his wife did have a son, and as soon as Zechariah wrote down the baby's name - John - he could speak again! John grew up to be a special prophet who talked about Jesus and baptized many people!

Talk About: Do you have any cousins?

Prayer: Thank you for the people in my family!

11. Baptism of Jesus

Read: Matthew 3:13-17

Jesus walked to the Jordan River one day. This is where John the Baptist was baptizing people. Jesus came so that He could get baptized too. John thought that Jesus should baptize Him instead! He knew that Jesus was the Saviour that the Israelites had been waiting for, and He didn't feel important enough to do Jesus' baptism! But Jesus told John that it was OK, and it was the right thing to do, so John baptized Jesus.

People that get baptized sometimes get dunked under the water and lifted back up again - to represent God washing us clean from sin and having a new life that is full of forgiveness! As soon as Jesus came up out of the water, God sent a special sort of dove to rest on Jesus, and God's voice from heaven said, "This is my son, whom I love; with Him I am well pleased."

Talk About: Do you know anyone who has been baptized?

Prayer: God, help me to know when it's the right time for me to get baptized, and let my life be always pleasing to You.

12. Jesus in the Wilderness

Read: Luke 4:1-13

After John baptized Jesus, God led Jesus into the wilderness. There are no homes, stores, or schools in the wilderness. In fact, there is nothing but rocks and dirt in the wilderness! Jesus didn't eat anything for 40 days, and He was very hungry and tired. Can you imagine how Jesus was feeling?

That's when the devil showed up to try and trick Jesus into following him instead of God. The devil is the biggest bad guy of all time and he is also called Satan. Satan tried to trick Jesus three times, and every time Jesus remembered a Bible verse and defeated Satan's tricks by saying the verses. Then Jesus told Satan to go away and angels took care of Jesus. Jesus defeated the devil in the wilderness!

Talk About: How long was Jesus in the wilderness? How was Jesus feeling? Who came to trick Jesus? Who came to care for Jesus?

Prayer: Thank You God for the Bible. Help us to remember the words of truth in the Bible and help us keep the lies out of our hearts and minds.

13. First Miracle of Jesus

Read: John 2: 1-11

Jesus was at a wedding with his family and with some of the men who were starting to hang around with Jesus. These men were called disciples and they travelled around with Jesus, learning from the things He was teaching people about God, and helping Him with whatever He needed.

Wine was being served at the wedding, but then they ran out! Jesus' mother asked Him to do something about it, and He decided to do HIs first miracle! Jesus turned big jugs of water into big jugs of wine! Only the servants, Jesus' mother, and Jesus' disciples knew about what He'd done. This miracle made Jesus' disciples believe in Him even more than they already did. And the people at the wedding kept on having a great time at the party!

Talk About: Have you ever been to a wedding?

Prayer: I am looking forward to reading more about Jesus and all the amazing things he did during his life. I am excited to learn about more of his miracles and the things he taught about God.

14. Nicodemus

Read: John 3:1-3, 16-17

Nicodemus was an important Jewish teacher. He came to Jesus one night to talk with Him and ask questions. Nicodemus believed Jesus had come from God and could do miraculous things. Jesus talked to Nicodemus about living a life that follows God. It's like being born again. Not like being born when you are a baby, but living a new kind of life that pleases God. This kind of life means trying to do what God wants, instead of what we want. Sometimes we want the same things God wants, and then it's easy to follow Him! But sometimes we want different things, and then it can get a little hard. Jesus told Nicodemus that God sent Jesus to the world because He loves us and wants to be with us forever in heaven. When we believe in Jesus, and ask God to forgive all our sins (all the wrong things we do) that makes God and all the angels VERY happy!

Talk About: Why did God send Jesus to us? Can we live in heaven with him?

Prayer: God, I want to live in heaven with you one day!

15. Jesus Heals a Nobleman's Son

Read: John 4:46-54

Jesus' second miracle happened in the same town as the water into wine miracle. A Roman leader's son was sick and was going to die. The nobleman went to Jesus to ask Him to come to his house and heal his son. Instead of going with him, Jesus just told him, "Go your way; your son lives!"

As the Roman man was travelling home, one of his servants met him and told him, "Your son lives!" The Roman asked what time his son had gotten better, and when his servant told him the answer, he realized it was at the same time as Jesus had told him his son would live. WOW!

After that, the Roman man, and all of his family and his servants believed more and more in God.

Talk About: How did Jesus heal the boy when he wasn't even with him?

Prayer: You are so powerful that you can heal people even from far away! Thank you for all the times you have helped me in my life!

16. Four Fishermen Follow Jesus

Read: Luke 5:1-11

One day Jesus was standing by the Lake of Gennesaret, and he saw two fishing boats on shore. The fishermen were washing their nets, but Jesus stepped into Simon's boat and asked him to take the boat into the water. Simon told Jesus that after a long night of fishing, his crew hadn't caught any fish at all, but then he agreed to try again with Jesus. Well, this time the nets were so full of fish that they were breaking! They had to call for their partners (James and John) to help them bring in the catch! Now two boats were so full of fish that they began to sink!

Jesus asked Simon and his brother Andrew, and James and John to come and follow him. Right away they left everything (even all the fish they just caught) and followed Him.

Talk About: Have you ever been fishing?

Prayer: It is amazing that you can fill fishing nets where there were no fish! And it's amazing that people will leave everything to follow you!

17. Matthew Follows Jesus

Read: Mark 2:13-17

Jesus loved to walk by the lake, and usually crowds of people would ask him to speak to them and teach them about God. One day he was walking and saw a man named Levi (later he changed his name to Matthew) who was working at a tax collector's booth. Taxes are the money people have to pay to the leaders of a country. The leaders are supposed to use the money to make sure people are taken care of properly. But leaders often kept a lot of money just for themselves, and so people didn't like tax collectors very much. Jesus told Levi to get up from the table and follow Him. Levi did just that! It seemed so easy for some people to leave everything and go with Jesus!

Talk About: Do you have a nickname? Or does anyone call you by a different name sometimes?

Prayer: You can change people's lives so much that even their names change sometimes! Please change my life in good ways as I grow up and get older.

18. Jesus Chooses 12 Disciples

Read: Luke 6:12-16

Jesus went to a mountainside so that he could be alone and pray. He wanted to talk to God about who he should choose to be his disciples. Disciples are people that learn many things from a teacher or leader. These are special things that most people wouldn't learn. Jesus wanted to have 12 men with him that would follow him and learn much more about God from him. He wanted to make sure he chose the men God wanted him to choose, so he prayed all night before making a decision. Jesus picked these 12 men to be his disciples: Simon (he changed his name to Peter), Andrew, James, John, Philip, Bartholomew, Levi (he changed his name to Matthew), Thomas, James son of Alphaeus, Simon the Zealot, Judas son of James, and Judas Iscariot.

Talk About: Do you like making choices in your life? Is it hard for you or easy for you? Do you ask your parents to help you make choices?

Prayer: Thank you that we can pray to you and ask you to help us make choices in our lives.

19. Sermon on the Mount

Read: Matthew 5:1-11

Jesus loved to teach people about God. One of the most famous talks Jesus gave was called the Sermon on the Mount, and it actually happened on a mountainside! Jesus noticed there were crowds of people around him, and he knew it would be a great chance to talk to them about living for God. The Beatitudes were part of the talk - they are all about ways that we can be blessed by God. Jesus also talked about some of the ways we can show God's love to others, some of the consequences that might happen if we choose to do wrong things in our lives, and some of the things we can look forward to if we live for God. These were all fantastic lessons that Jesus gave to the crowds that day!

Talk About: What are consequences?

Prayer: Thank you for all the talks and lessons that Jesus gave in the Bible. We can learn so much from Him!

20. Parables of Jesus

Read: Matthew 13: 1-9, 18-23

One of the best ways Jesus knew to teach people about God was to tell them "parables". Parables were stories Jesus used in his lessons, and they had special meanings in them.

There was one day that Jesus told many parables all at the same time. He told them to some large crowds that gathered around him by a lake. He actually got into a boat and spoke to them from out on the water so they could hear him better! Some of the parables Jesus told were called The Sower, The Weeds, The Mustard Seed, The Hidden Treasure and The Pearl, and The Net. These parables helped people understand more about God because Jesus was using examples about farming and fishing. A lot of the people in the crowds worked at those jobs for a living.

Talk About: What is a parable? What jobs do your parents do for a living?

Prayer: I love stories, God! And I love these stories for Lent that are all about the life of Jesus. I love learning more about him!

21. Jesus Calms the Storm

Read: Mark 4:35-41

After telling the crowds the parables by the lake, Jesus asked his disciples to go with him in a boat to the other side of the lake, where it would be quiet and they could get some rest.

Jesus was so tired that he fell asleep in the boat! Then a terrible storm started up as they were rowing. The waves were crashing over the side of the boat, but Jesus kept on sleeping on his cushion. The disciples were in a panic and they woke Jesus up to help them. Jesus simply stood up and told the wind and waves to "Quiet! Be still!" The storm calmed down completely and the boat sailed peacefully to the other side. The disciples were starting to get an idea of just how amazing Jesus was by all the teachings he gave and the miracles he did!

Talk About: Have you ever been outside in a storm?

Prayer: Storms are scary, God. Sometimes scary things or sad things or bad things can happen in life. It is good to know you are always there.

22. Nazareth Turns Against Jesus

Read: Mark 6:1-6

Jesus decided to visit his hometown in Nazareth. He took his disciples with him. They went to the temple and Jesus started teaching the people about God. The audience was amazed at the things he knew, and the miracles he did. They wondered where he got all his wisdom and power. They knew him as the son of Joseph, the carpenter. His mother was Mary, his brothers were James, Joseph, Judas, and Simon, and his sisters still lived in town. This is what they knew about Jesus.

The people of Nazareth were not happy with the changes in Jesus, and they didn't have much faith in him at all. So Jesus didn't do very many miracles while he was there. He loves it when people believe in him and the power of God in him to do miracles.

Talk About: What do we do when our friends or family don't want to hear about God?

Prayer: Even if people don't want to hear about you, God, I pray that I will never stop following you and your plan for my life.

23. Jesus Sends out the 12

Read: Luke 9: 1-6

Jesus passed along many of his powers to the 12 special disciples he had chosen. They were given some of Jesus' powers to heal sick people and make evil go away.

One day Jesus sent the 12 disciples on a journey to tell more people about God and help them with sickness and other troubles. He gave special instructions to his disciples for their journey. He told them to take nothing - no walking stick or backpack or food or money or extra clothes! Can you imagine going on a vacation with no luggage at all? Jesus told them to stay wherever people would invite them into their homes, and leave the town if no one invited them in. These instructions seemed to work and many people came to know more about God from the disciples' journey.

Talk About: Have you ever gone on a long trip? What did you take with you?

Prayer: Wherever I go, you are there. I know that you take care of all of us. I also know we need to take care of each other.

24. Jesus Feeds Thousands!

Read: Matthew 14:13-21

Jesus heard about his cousin John's death and was very sad. He wanted to be alone, but crowds of people followed him to hear him talk about God. Jesus "had compassion on them and healed their sick."

It became very late in the day and the crowds did not want to go home, but everyone was getting hungry. Jesus told the disciples to feed the people, but they could only find 5 loaves of bread and 2 fish. Jesus took the food, looked up to heaven, gave thanks to God, and broke the bread. It was a miracle - the disciples just kept handing out the food to the hungry people, and the food never ran out. More than 5000 men, women and children ate plenty that day. There was even 12 baskets of food left over!

Talk About: How did Jesus feed thousands of people from 5 loaves of bread and 2 fish - PLUS have 12 baskets of food left over?

Prayer: God, you can do anything! You can work amazing miracles! You can feed the whole world if only we share a little of what we have. Thank you!

25. Jesus Walks on Water

Read: John 6: 16-24

The same night that Jesus fed more than 5000 people, his disciples got into a boat and set off across the lake. They were going to a town called Capernaum.

It was dark and Jesus hadn't come with them. A strong wind came up and the water grew rough. All of a sudden Jesus was coming towards them - walking on the water! The disciples were very afraid because they thought they were seeing a ghost! But Jesus told them not to worry, and they let him come into the boat. Jesus and the disciples made it safely to the other side of the lake.

Talk About: Have you ever been in a boat? What would happen if you tried to walk on the water?

Prayer: You are full of surprises and it will be exciting to get to know you throughout my whole life! I can't wait to see what you will do next!

26. Jesus Says He Will Die Soon

Read: Matthew 16:21-28

Jesus was a very special man - the most special man that ever lived on earth. He was the Son of God after all! He could do things that most people can't do, and he knew things that most people don't know.

Jesus knew when he was going to die and how it was going to happen. He started to tell his disciples about this because he wanted to prepare them for what was coming. Jesus knew he would suffer because of some Jewish leaders that were very confused about him. They didn't know that he was the Son of God. Jesus also knew he was going to come back to life 3 days after he was killed. Imagine knowing all those things about your life before they ever happened!

Talk About: What do you think you might be when you grow up?

Prayer: I know you have a good plan for my life, God. Please show me what it is as I grow up and get older. I will always try to follow your plan for me.

27. Jesus Transforms on the Mountain

Read: Mark 9:2-9

After a few days Jesus led 3 of his disciples - Peter, James and John - on a walk with him up a high mountain. There was no one else around. Suddenly Jesus changed right before their eyes! His face was shining like a beautiful bright light and his clothes became "dazzling white, whiter than anyone in the world could bleach them." And 2 men also appeared - Elijah and Moses - these were great leaders from the olden days in the Bible. They were visiting Jesus from heaven! Elijah and Moses talked with Jesus for a while, and then disappeared. Then a cloud appeared and a voice said "This is my Son, whom I love. Listen to him!" And then the disciples were alone with Jesus once more. What amazing things happened on the mountain! These were things that don't happen very often in the Bible. Jesus was getting ready for something special, and he needed a lot of encouragement and support from God and other strong men of faith.

Talk About: What is the nicest thing anyone has ever said to you?

Prayer: Help me say kind words to people and not words that would hurt.

28. Jesus Sends Out the 72

Read: Luke 10:1-11

Remember how Jesus sent out his 12 disciples to tell people about God? Well, now he was sending out 72. He wanted them to go out into the country and visit some towns. Jesus would be travelling to that part of the country soon and wanted to know which towns would be the best to visit and tell people about God. Jesus told the 72 followers to go in twos and they were not to take anything with them.

Jesus gave them instructions about staying at houses where they were invited, and not moving around too much. He also told them to teach people about God and heal the sick people, and report back about how the visits went. Jesus was hoping that sending out 72 would help spread God's message of love and peace much further than if he was to try it alone.

Talk About: Do you think 72 people could visit many towns in a short time?

Prayer: I ask you for some friends who believe in you, God, so that we can learn more about you together.

29. Jesus Attends A Feast

Read: John 7:1-5, 10-15

There were many special holidays that were celebrated in the Jewish land where Jesus grew up. One of the holidays was the Feast of Tabernacles, and it lasted for a whole week! This was a celebration of harvest time and a remembrance of the way God took care of the Jewish people as they wandered in the desert for 40 years. This was after they had been Egyptian slaves for hundreds of years, and before they entered the promised land.

Jesus' brothers wanted him to go to the feast with them and celebrate, but Jesus wanted to go and teach more people about God. So, he snuck in a few days after the feast started. When Jesus spoke to the people, they were amazed at his wisdom.

Talk About: What is your favourite holiday?

Prayer: There are so many things to celebrate in our lives, God. Every day can be a celebration of something good that you bring to us.

30. Jesus Raises Lazarus From Dead

Read: John 11:1-23, 32-44

Jesus had a good friend named Lazarus - his sisters were Mary and Martha. Jesus loved this whole family very much. One day Jesus was told that Lazarus was very sick, but Jesus did not go to help him right away. He had a better plan. After 2 days Jesus travelled to Lazarus, but Jesus knew Lazarus had already died. Everyone was very sad about the death of Lazarus and they wondered why Jesus hadn't come sooner to help. Jesus cried about the sad situation and the hurt his friends were feeling. But he had a better plan, and he went to the grave of Lazarus. Jesus told them to roll away the stone from in front of Lazarus' tomb, and then he told Lazarus to come out! AND HE DID! It was a miracle! This is what Jesus wanted to happen all along, so that people would see God's great power.

Talk About: Have you ever been very sick?

Prayer: Thank you that you have so much power to heal the sick people in our world. Please heal the sick people that I know today. They are….

31. Jesus Spends Time Alone with God

Read: Mark 1:35 & 6:46

Jesus loved to spend time alone with God. He would wake up before everyone else and go out to find a quiet spot to talk to God. He seemed to especially like going to mountains to pray. Maybe Jesus felt closer to God that way, maybe it was very quiet on the mountainsides, or maybe there was a lot of beauty in the nature around him on the mountains. Maybe it was all those things. Jesus knew it was important to pray and listen to God. Listening to God just means being quiet sometimes when we pray. God might help us start to think about how much we love someone, or how we can help someone, or how much God loves us. We might get some great ideas as we try to listen to God. Jesus always prayed when he was making big decisions like choosing his 12 special disciples or when he had a big job to do.

Talk About: Where is your favourite place to pray?

Prayer: Thank you God that we can talk to you anytime, anywhere, about anything! It is so good to know you are listening. Help me listen to you.

32. The Great Commandments

Read: Matthew 22:35-40

An Israelite priest was standing in the crowds surrounding Jesus one day. He wanted to test how much Jesus knew about God. The priest asked Jesus a question, "What is the greatest commandment in the Law?" (OR What is the most important rule in the Bible?). Jesus answered, "Love the Lord your God with all your heart and with all your soul and with all your mind. This is the first and greatest commandment. And the second is like it: Love your neighbour as yourself." These are the two most amazing ways we can follow God in our lives. Love Him most of all, and love others at least as much as we love ourselves. That also means caring for others as much as we care for ourselves - like making sure others have things they need to have a healthy life, or helping them be happy, or telling them God loves them.

Talk About: What is the greatest commandment? And the second greatest?

Prayer: God, I want to love you most in my life. And I want to love others second. Keep on teaching me how to do those two most important things.

33. We Need to Really Love Them...

Read: Matthew 25:31-45

Jesus was talking with his disciples one day and he told them a story about sheep and goats. He said that some people who follow God are like sheep, and some are like goats. The people who are like sheep know that it's very important to help others in our lives. The people who are like goats don't really understand how important that is. Jesus said he will want the "sheep" to be with him in heaven. These are some people Jesus wants us to help:

- Hungry, thirsty, strangers (Matthew 25:35)
- Those without clothes, sick, prisoners (Matthew 25:36)
- Orphans and widows (James 1:27)
- Poor, blind, and oppressed (Luke 4:18)
- The lost (Luke 19:10)
- Crippled and lame (Luke 14:13)
- Lepers and deaf (Matthew 11:5)

Talk About: Which group of people would you like to help? How?

Prayer: Help me to love the people you want me to love. Show me how, God.

34. The Parable of the Good Samaritan

Read: Luke 10:25-37

A priest asked Jesus about the best way to follow God and make sure to live in heaven one day. The priest thought the answer was to love God and love our neighbours. Jesus told the priest he was right and then told a story about who our neighbours are.

The story talks about a Jewish man who was robbed while travelling. He was beaten up and left on the road. A priest walked by and didn't help the man, then a church worker walked by and didn't help the injured man either. The next man that walked by was a Samaritan. At that time Samaritans were usually enemies to the Jews, but this man was caring and kind. He helped the Jewish man - he took care of his wounds, put him on his donkey and took him to a place where he could get better. He paid for all the Jewish man's medicine and food.

Talk About: Do you think you would have helped the injured man on the road?

Prayer: Help me to even love my enemies, God!

35. Jesus Washes the Disciples' Feet

Read: John 13:1-17

Jesus was having dinner with his disciples one night and he wanted to do something special for them. He got up and wrapped a towel around his waist, poured water into a bowl, and started washing his disciple's feet. Then he dried their feet with the towel. Jesus even washed the feet of a disciple who he knew would treat him very badly very soon (but that's another story). Peter didn't want Jesus to wash his feet - usually this job was for the lowest servant in the house. Jesus told Peter that even though they were disciples, they would still need to keep cleaning all the sin out of their hearts to keep following God. Jesus was also trying to teach the disciples that we have to help one another and do things for one another, and not worry about who is the best or the greatest.

Talk About: Have you ever washed anyone's feet? How can we keep cleaning sin out of our hearts?

Prayer: Please show me some kind things I can do for my friends & family.

36. Jesus Blesses the Children

Read: Luke 18:15-16

Jesus loved children. I can picture him enjoying the children around him wherever he went - tickling them, holding their fingers as they took their first steps, rocking them to sleep, or telling them stories on His lap. He knew they were the hope and the future of the world.

One day people were bringing babies and children to Jesus so that he could bless them. The disciples tried to tell people not to bring the children to Jesus since he was so busy with other things, but Jesus said he wanted to be with the children. Jesus said that everyone should believe in God the way that children do - with their whole hearts. And everyone should love one another the way that children do - with no limits. Children (that means YOU!) have a lot to teach us about God. It's not always the other way around!

Talk About: If Jesus were there with you, what would you like to do with him? Play a game, read a book, go for a walk, dance, sing, or just talk?

Prayer: Show me how we can spend time together today God!

37. Zacchaeus Climbs a Tree

Read: Luke 19:1-10

There is a song that goes "Zacchaeus was a wee little man, and a wee little man was he. He climbed up in a sycamore tree, for the Lord he wanted to see."

That song is Zacchaeus' story. He was one of the chief tax collectors and he was very rich. He really wanted to see Jesus, but he was so small that he couldn't see Jesus in the crowds. So he climbed a tree to see Jesus, and that's when Jesus saw him. Jesus wanted to come to Zacchaeus' house for dinner, and this made Zacchaeus very happy. Zacchaeus decided right then and there to give away half of his things to people who were poor, and pay back anyone he had ever cheated in taxes. In fact he would pay them back 4 times the amount he cheated them! Jesus was very pleased with Zacchaeus.

Talk About: Do you like to climb trees? What do you see when you climb?

Prayer: I would climb trees and mountains, and swim across rivers to see you!

38. Jesus Arrives at Bethany

Read: John 11:55 - 12:1

Every spring the Jewish people had a festival called Passover. This festival was a celebration of God freeing the Israelites from 400 years of slavery to the Egyptians. Passover lasted about a week, and Jews from all over the world travelled to Jerusalem to celebrate. People were looking for Jesus at the Passover one year - they wanted to see him and hear him talk about God. But some of the Jewish leaders had told people to tell them if they saw Jesus, because they wanted to arrest him! They thought that Jesus was getting too much attention for all his miracles and teachings. They thought too many people were starting to follow Jesus and not follow them anymore. They were getting pretty angry at Jesus. But Jesus came to the Passover anyway, and stopped in Bethany first. This is the place where Jesus raised Lazarus from the dead.

Talk About: Have you ever had anyone get really mad at you?

Prayer: If people get mad at me, help me to keep showing them your love.

39. The Sabbath

There are no Bible readings for today. This day is not really mentioned in the Gospels. The gospels are the 4 books of the Bible that talk about Jesus' life—Matthew, Mark, Luke and John.

For the Jews, today was a Sabbath day. That means people were sitting and resting - they did this once every week. What a good idea! Jesus had been travelling around the country for 3 years now, telling people about God, healing the sick, performing other miracles, and teaching the disciples. He had walked about 5000 kilometres altogether - that's almost like walking across the whole country of Canada! Before Jesus turned 30, he mostly stayed in his hometown. In the last 3 years, when Jesus was ages 30-33, he walked all around ancient Israel and visited many cities.

Talk About: How do you think Jesus was feeling after all the travelling?

Prayer: Thank you for days of rest and relaxation. Thank you for special times we get to spend with family and friends - just enjoying life.

40. Holy Week Begins - Palm Sunday

Read: Mark 11:1-11

Jesus and his disciples travelled to Jerusalem for the Jewish festival of Passover. Jesus knew there were many people waiting to see him in the city - some would be happy to see him, and some would try to hurt him. He wanted to enter the city in a special way, but what he did was not like most famous people. He sent 2 of his disciples to get a donkey in a nearby village. He knew exactly where the donkey would be, and he knew that no one had ever ridden the donkey before. The owners let the disciples have the donkey as soon as they found out it was for Jesus. People spread their coats and some palm branches on the road ahead of Jesus. He rode the donkey as he entered Jerusalem. The people shouted "Hosanna!" (means save).

Talk About: Did you know that donkeys have the markings of a cross on their backs?

Prayer: Jesus was so brave to go to a place where people might be waiting to hurt him. Help me to be brave when I'm in a scary or confusing place.

41. Monday - Jesus Clears the Temple

Read: Mark 11:15-18

Jesus decided to walk into the temple (church) in Jerusalem. He couldn't believe what he was seeing when he walked in there! People were selling things to each other at crazy prices and trying to get rich from those that followed God.

Jesus got really upset and flipped over tables and told the sellers to leave at once. He reminded everyone that the temple was God's house and it was supposed to be a holy place of prayer for the world. It was not supposed to be a place to try and make money and cheat people with crazy prices. Also, this same day the Jewish leaders started making plans to kill Jesus because they didn't understand he was trying to help people follow God.

Talk About: Do you like going to church? Why or why not?

Prayer: God, thank you for churches and other places where people get together to learn more about you.

42. Tuesday - Two Coins

Read: Mark 12:41-44

Every day during the Passover festival Jesus went to the temple to teach people about God. Then at night he would go to the Mount of Olives to teach there. He was always trying to help people follow God. One day he was sitting in the temple near the place where people put their money offerings. He noticed rich people throwing in large amounts, and then he noticed a poor widow who gave two very small coins. Jesus told his disciples that this woman gave more than all the others because she gave everything she had to live on. Now she had no money for food or anything else, and she was going to trust God to take care of her somehow. The rich people knew they had more money at home, but the widow gave all her money to God.

Talk About: Have you ever given money away? How did it feel if you did?

Prayer: Help me remember the widow's two coins whenever it seems hard to give something away to someone.

43. Wednesday-Perfume Poured on Jesus

Read: Mark 14:3-9

Today was a day of rest for Jesus and the disciples. They were staying at a friend's house in Bethany. One night they were having dinner and a woman came over to Jesus and poured perfume on him! This perfume was very expensive, and some of the people there couldn't believe that this woman had just poured it out on Jesus! They thought this was a waste because the perfume could have been sold for lots of money to give to the poor. Jesus told them to leave the woman alone - he thought she had done a beautiful thing. In those days, people who had died were covered in oils and perfumes and spices when they were buried. Jesus knew that soon he would die and be buried. He thought it was so nice that the woman was trying to show love to him.

Talk About: How much money do you think the perfume cost?

Prayer: Please give me ideas to do really nice things for my family and friends. And help me to actually do them.

44. Thursday-Communion & the Garden

Read: Mark 14:12-26, 32-41

Many things happened on this day of Jesus' life! This was the night of the Passover meal in the Jewish festival. Jesus and his disciples found a quiet room to have their meal. The first communion happened at this meal. Communion is when Christians eat and drink special things (usually bread and grape juice) to remind them of Jesus and all he did for us. They also pray and read the Bible.

After the Passover meal, they went to the Garden of Gethsemane. Jesus prayed a lot that night, alone with God in the garden. He knew the next couple of days were going to be very hard.

Then Jesus was arrested! One of his own disciples (Judas) turned him over to the Jewish leaders that wanted to kill him! This must have broken Jesus' heart—that a friend would do that to him.

Talk About: Have you ever been hurt by a good friend? How did it feel?

Prayer: Help me to forgive my friends when they hurt my feelings, and help me not to hurt my friends' feelings.

45. Good Friday - Crucifixion

Read: Luke 23:13-25, 32-49

Jesus was brought to Pilate to get charged as a criminal. Many of the Jewish leaders and the people wanted Jesus to be killed for saying he was the Son of God. Many people didn't believe him.

Pilate didn't want to kill Jesus, but he let the Jews decide. Jesus was sentenced to be killed along with two other criminals. All three men would be hung on crosses - this was how they killed many prisoners at that time. Pilate wanted a sign hung above Jesus that said "King of the Jews". One of the criminals who was on the cross next to Jesus chose to follow God that day, even though he was dying. Jesus told him he would be in heaven with God that very day. Jesus was even saving people as he was dying! He asked God to forgive the people that had killed him, and then he died.

Talk About: What do you think Jesus was feeling on the cross?

Prayer: I'm not sure how to say thank you for sending someone to give their life for me, God. That is the greatest thing and I love you.

46. Saturday - Jesus in the Tomb

Read: Matthew 27:57-66

After Jesus died on Good Friday, one of his followers named Joseph of Arimathea put Jesus' body in a new tomb that he had cut out of the rock for himself. He wrapped Jesus' body in a clean sheet and rolled a large stone across the entrance of the tomb. Two of Jesus' followers who were women (and both named Mary) sat outside the tomb for a while.

The Jewish leaders went to Pilate because they were afraid the disciples would steal Jesus' body. They remembered Jesus had said he would come back to life after 3 days, and they didn't want the disciples to trick people into believing that. So Pilate sent guards to watch over the entrance of the tomb.

Talk About: Why did Pilate send guards to watch over the tomb of Jesus?

What is going to happen to Jesus?

Prayer: Help me to remember that Easter Sunday is coming tomorrow, and something truly special happened on the first Easter Sunday!

47. Easter Sunday - Resurrection

Read: Matthew 28:1-16

It was still dark on Sunday morning when both the Marys went to visit Jesus' tomb again. Suddenly the ground shook like an earthquake and an angel from heaven rolled the stone away from the entrance to the tomb! The angel looked as bright as lightning with clothes white as snow.

The guards at the tomb were very afraid, and they went to tell the Jewish leaders what happened. The leaders gave them lots of money so they would lie and tell people the disciples took Jesus' body.

Meanwhile at the tomb, the angel said to the women, "Don't be afraid. Jesus is not here, he is risen just like he said he would. Look in the tomb, then go and tell the disciples what has happened. Jesus will meet them in Galilee." The women ran to tell the disciples the good news. On the way, Jesus himself met them and talked to them. They were so happy!

Talk About: How can Jesus be alive again after dying on a cross?

Prayer: Thank you for all that Jesus did for me at Easter time!!

48. Easter Monday

Read: Mark 16:9-20

Jesus appeared to many people after he rose from the dead. First the Marys and then two men walking on a country road. Both times the disciples were told about it, but they didn't believe the news! Then Jesus appeared to the disciples himself and they finally believed he had come back to life. They were very happy!

Jesus told the disciples he wanted them to go out into the whole world and teach people how to follow God with all their hearts.

40 days after Jesus rose from the dead he did something else that was absolutely amazing. He told his disciples he would be with them always, then he rose up into the sky and went on to heaven! It was time for him to be with God again. And it was time for Jesus' followers to start telling more people about God.

Talk About: What did Jesus tell his disciples to do?

Prayer: Help me to remember everything I learned about Jesus during Lent!

About the Author

Anna loves to make easy-to-use resources for the family that encourage a more simple life and a chance to truly live in the moments of each day.

She enjoys life in Northern Ontario with her husband & two growing sons.

Anna loves to read, write, weave, quilt, bake, walk, and bicycle.

More From Anna

Simply Live Blog—*annasklar.ca*

Etsy Shop—SklarInk—*etsy.com/ca/shop/SklarInk*

OTHER RESOURCES BY ANNA

2017 Bible in a Year Journal *(with daily reading suggestions & blank space to write, doodle, or draw)*
Paperback (Amazon), Digital Download (Etsy)

The Jesus Tree—48 Family Devotions for Lent
*Paperback (Amazon), eBook (Kindle),
Digital Download (Etsy)*

The Jesse Tree Series for Advent
Paperback (Amazon), Digital Download (Etsy):

28 Family Devotions *(also on Kindle)*

28 Colouring Pages

28 Ornaments with Family Devotions & Illustrations

Lunchbox LOL Series
Paperback (Amazon), Digital Download (Etsy):

200 Jokes for the Lunchbox

200 Silly Questions for the Lunchbox

200 Days of Word Play for the Lunchbox

200 Calculator Word Games for the Lunchbox

200 Fun Facts & Trivia for the Lunchbox

200 Riddles for the Lunchbox

200 Holiday Jokes

Complete Lunchbox LOL Series

The Princess of Dreams *(a children's story)*
Paperback (Amazon), eBook (Kindle)

Thy Word—A Journal of Reading Through the Bible in a Year
Paperback (Amazon), eBook (Kindle)

Discovering Hope—Sharing the Journey of Healing After Miscarriage, Stillbirth, or Infant Loss
Paperback (Amazon), eBook (Kindle)

Made in the USA
Middletown, DE
13 March 2017